The Solex Brothers (Redux)

LUKE KENNARD is a poet, critic, dramatist and pugilist. He is compassionate, but prone to anxiety and bleak introspection. Many have called him polite and quite funny, but add that he suffers from a tendency towards constant nervous laughter and an apparently involuntary rictus of disdain. His poetry and criticism have appeared in *Stride Magazine*, *Sentence*, *Echo:Location*, *The Tall Lighthouse Review*, *Reactions 4*, *Orbis*, *14 Magazine*, *The Flying Post*, *Exultations and Difficulties*. He won an Eric Gregory Award in 2005 and was shortlisted for the Forward Prize in 2007. He is quite tall.

Also by Luke Kennard

The Harbour Beyond the Movie (Salt Publishing, 2007, 2010)
The Migraine Hotel (Salt Publishing, 2009)

The Solex Brothers (Redux)

And Other Prose Poems

Now with explanatory notes

Luke Kennard

London

PUBLISHED BY SALT PUBLISHING
Dutch House, 307–308 High Holborn, London WC1V 7LL United Kingdom

First published by Stride Publications 2005
Second edition Salt Publishing 2007
This paperback edition Salt Publishing 2010

Printed and bound in the United Kingdom by Biddles Ltd, Kings Lynn, Norfolk

Typeset in Swift 9.5 / 13

ISBN 978 1 84471 411 7 hardback
ISBN 978 1 84471 548 0 paperback

Salt Publishing Ltd gratefully acknowledges
the financial assistance of Arts Council England

1 3 5 7 9 8 6 4 2

For Zoë

Contents

Acknowledgements

The author wishes to thank Rupert M. Loydell, editor of Stride Books, for his permission to reprint the text of *The Solex Brothers* (Stride Books, 2005) in this new edition. And, more to the point, for publishing it in the first place.

Andy Brown for constant encouragement, inspiration and clear-sighted criticism.

Somerset County Council, in whose offices and on whose scrap paper many of these poems began. The Eric Gregory Foundation and The Society of Authors for an award in 2005.

The Solex Brothers

I

I boarded the train. 'It's great, the way you use your feet to play that guitar,' I said. We were all given water, a gesture some interpreted as political and, on grounds of having no interest in politics, refused to drink. 'Fools,' muttered the politician. 'Politics is in my hair. Politics is seeping out of my pores.'

The train mounted a bridge over the sea. Tiny blue swallows decorated us. I shared a cabin with an undercover policeman and the Solex Brothers, twice the size of ordinary men. The Solex Brothers were broad and salient, their card game a distraction. I had heard about them: 'They grab you by the head and force your head into places it doesn't normally go—like into a jug.'

Oh, cruel freewill. Every year I make this journey for reasons *known* but unfathomable, my mouth tight with disdain. Yesterday I overwound my watch and the spring snapped with a cavernous sound. I wish I'd never offered them a cognac, but we are damned to believe a man when he tells us we are kind: the half that doesn't believe him is relieved.

'Marbles,' said the undercover policeman, producing a bag and spilling them onto the floor. In the ensuing chaos, we alighted on our knees.

II

On Platform 4 the Solex Brothers ran this way and that, chasing the shapes of women. They had no luggage, but a Mustang idled to convey them hence. 'Ride with us, why don't you?' they cried.

I fell asleep in the leatherette silence. I dreamt I was a liar. I awoke to see turquoise light rushing between the branches. A sandwich board lay at the road side.

'Give us a song!' cried the Solex Brothers. And to my relief I found they were talking to the chauffeur. A deer sprung over the road.

'Fields of inedible vegetables,' sang the chauffeur, 'midden boys tainting their flocks. Songs anti- and pro- all have dead melodies; for tuppence I'll show you my scar.'

And we all joined in the second time:

Fields of inedible vegetables,
Midden boys, tainting their flocks,
Songs anti- and pro- all have dead melodies,
For tuppence I'll show you my scar.

And the chauffeur sang the next verse:

Shields of gentle Euripides,
Hidden joys wait in your docks,
Throngs come and go, but the static will grow,
For instance, when driving a car.

'It's a chauffeur song,' he explained. 'You know, for the Little Guy.' The roadside diners glimmered like bookshelves, little glowing bookshelves.

III

The ecstatic chariots in my lungs.

'These are your quarters, dear boy, above the library. Those are the moors, this is the bread room, overhead the incident hallway—avoid that if possible.'

'And in that room is young Lucida, a prodigy—whom we have engaged you to teach.' The other Solex brother laughed. 'She is beautiful as a summer evening,' he yelled.

I was to teach Lucida the works of Pushkin.

I attended to ablutions, marvelling that I had been employed in so happy a capacity. Not once had I made this journey and found work that agreed with me as much as lecturing a beautiful young woman on the works of Pushkin.

As I lathered my face and weighed the golden razor in my hand, a bell rang like a crystal and I cut my face several times so as not to be late.

Dressed in my new suit, I took three stairs at a time, scarcely able to contain etc.

But to my horror, Lucida—who I met over dinner—turned out to be a rag doll made of dish-cloths.

IV

There were no words in the library. Sometimes their lectures were just butterflies released into the theatre; the prevalence of butterflies, their silence.

Under the tutelage of the Solex Brothers I learned that in all things, there is a kite—whether caked in silence or snagged on promise.

Their house, lodged in a valley, caught fire frequently due to the thin air.

Each day at twelve we ate national dishes. At dinner, a thin gruel called *skirmish*.

I soon swore off parataxis—its fragments of mistrust.

Behind a locked door they kept an inverted castle, a red ceramic affair, decorated with hysterical curlicues and loops that went on to form part of the structure. A black a hole in its side.

I put my head into the thing and something marvellous happened. It was dark and cold and my headache siphoned off, into the thing, and never troubled me again.

Landscape with Mist and Devils was painted here.

We were visited with no little frequency by its painter, Emily Easterville. Her favourite outfit was a lake in the grounds of the house. She would stand in the middle of the lake, water up to her shoulders, and say, 'Help me get all these fish out of my dress.'

Underwater the kites flew.

V

What lurid adoption the Solex Brothers practised. A voice, foreign and new in the hall each morning. I lay in bed, afraid until the afternoon. Their cars left at exactly 8:30. I did the washing up in very hot water.

For a month I was happy in their patronage, happy in my solidity and in my arrogance, not to say innocence. I flexed my shoulders; I admired my shoulders in the deep yellow mirrors.

The Solex Brothers lived at some height, but the intricacy of their illustrations began to leave me jealous and dejected. That shameful dressing gown was always hanging somewhere in my mind, keeping me silent.

And I felt less welcome at the table—was always asked to, 'Go and help Lucida with the washing up. That girl hasn't stopped talking about you all day.'

So, festooned with cigarettes, I came to resent their sleek dispensations, came to loath their boring, tidal breath. My hands blistered and chafed for them.

I collected bread from the bakery. The Father, on his bicycle, whispered, 'A friend of mine would like a word with you.'

VI

It was not I who suggested murder—after all, other than employing me as protégé and butler, what was their crime?

But in the apple-strewn antechamber of the half-ruined church I learned that the Solex Brothers had made many enemies among the townsfolk.

'My vegetables may be inedible,' said Jack Glass, an arable farmer, 'but there are seven different varieties and they all have their uses.'

They had upset filing systems and undermined the quartz mine by building another mine underneath it.

'They killed my father and called it collateral damage,' said Sophie, a young woman the like of which I had hoped to lecture on Pushkin.

During a brief stint as mayors in 1978, the Solex Brothers had devolved every street in the city until it had its own jurisdiction and parliament. When they retired three years later, the new mayor attempted to reinstate what he saw as common sense, but, due to innumerable insolvencies since devolution, only $\frac{3}{8}$ of the streets wanted to be recentralised. The entire community, if you could call it that, was left in chaos.

But what of all their visitors and friends?

'Nonsense,' said the Father. 'Their visitors are paid actors—each brother takes it in turn to hire.'

As I had access to the meals of the Solex Brothers, it was decided that I should poison the *skirmish* and ring the crystal bell five times to let the city know of their demise.

'A person who does just what he or she has been told to do, and takes no real interest, will certainly not advance quickly,' said Sophie, handing me a leather-bound volume entitled *The Follies of The Solex Brothers, 1958–2002*.

VII

No sooner had I struck the crystal bell for the fifth time with the little wooden harlequin than I realised the poison in the *skirmish* had not slain the Solex Brothers. They sat up in their chairs and wiped the *skirmish* from their faces, blinking.

As fireworks burst over the city I clasped my brow in exasperation.

But my fortune was to turn for, while the poison had not ended the Solex Brothers, it had drained them of any sense forever.

'Few roads on the island are wide enough,' said one of the Solex Brothers.

'There are many brown bears in America,' said his brother.

'There are not many clouds now,' agreed the first Solex brother.

'I myself do not expect the Company ever to look back again,' said his brother.

'The time is come to receive it,' granted his brother.

'The wolverine trap will take too long to build,' his brother complained.

'She was most attractive in her scarlet bonnet,' said his brother. 'We shall be called The Snow People, I think.'

They wrote many poems over the next few days—and I oversaw this work and offered advice, taking pleasure in the cruel reversal. Their best was a three line poem without a title:

How beautiful the tops of the mountains are,
The red sun above them.
I don't understand anything about it.

VIII

I left town on the same train under a banner of knowledge. I had asked Sophie to accompany me, but she declined. The Solex Brothers gave a moving, harmless speech.

'I've learned so much from all of you,' I said, my lips pressed to the cold glass.

A man was still playing the guitar with his feet, but this time I didn't comment.

A journey back should always be underwritten.

EPILOGUE

He handed me the telephone. 'It is the Solex Brothers,' he said.

I indicated that I was not to be disturbed, but he wandered into the kitchen, shaking his head.

'If this is about the poison,' I said. But it was not about poison.

'Why does God allow us to suffer?' they asked.

Over the last year the Solex Brothers had come to rely on me for encouragement and edification.

'I don't know,' I said. 'Why does he allow us to feel joy?'

Outside the sea lapped the shore. I was trying this new water-flavour chewing gum.

About gum my grandmother said, 'You can chew that stuff as long as you don't chew it anywhere near me.' She said hundreds of more important things, too.

You lose everyone. Each loss prepares you for a greater loss. She didn't say that. That wasn't really her style.

'Hey,' said the Solex Brothers, noticing the silence, 'hey, are you *chewing* something? And what's with that flatmate of yours, anyway? I don't think he likes us. What are you supposed to do when someone doesn't like you?'

'Kill them,' I said.

The line went dead

To a Wolf

I

When I wrote to the wolf my tie got stuck in the pillar box. I waved my arms and screamed, 'Who! Whooooo!'

In my more fanciful moments I LIKE TO IMAGINE A TINY MAN inside the pillar box and I LIKE TO IMAGINE HIM HOLDING ONTO MY TIE FOR 'DEAR LIFE' as I wave my arms and try to pull myself away from the pillar box which I imagine HE, for whatever reason, WANTS TO PULL MY FACE VERY CLOSE TO, PERHAPS IN ORDER TO SPIT IN IT.

I had to remove my tie to free my body from the pillar box.

Anyway, my letter was lost in the post and it was months before I heard from the wolf. Wounded, he assumed I had neglected him:

Dear Bastard,

Nobody came to see the great show in the arboretum, in spite of free tickets attached to balloons and let loose over the city. Let us take a moment to imagine that:

Nobody.

Balloons!

Yrs,

Wolf

Sometimes I just stand at the top of the tower and I look all over the city and I weep about it. (Although really I am weeping about something else).

II

'You can keep your opinions and your achievements,' avers the wolf. 'Keep also your *raison d'etres* and your holidays. What I like are *representations of myself.*'

The wolf is just crazy for representations of himself.

'Here's a picture of you, wolf.'

'Great!' cries the wolf.

'Here's a story about you.'

'Give it here!' cries the wolf.

The arboretum has grown over with scathing moss. Inside members of staff have been asked to remain calm while the flowers grow over their uniform and pin them to the glass wall. Twenty members of staff, boys and girls, and one enormous uniform—so as they look not unlike a monster with many heads and limbs.

'I was told, come spring, we would all drink lamb's milk,' mutters the concierge. 'But *now* look at us.'

I spend November building a zoetrope that depicts the wolf standing on his hind legs and chasing a hoop.

'That's the most beautiful thing I've ever seen!' the wolf exclaims.

We could all stand to learn something from the wolf.

'Hey!' yelps the wolf, later. 'This novel you wrote about me is rather circumlocutory. Where are all the descriptions of my *white-noise* fur and bloody breath like the steam from a kettle?'

'It isn't finished yet,' I snap.

III

Today was a good day, but it was not the best day. Not a pirate ship or a bottle of invisible ink or a conversation with your friend in Morse Code. No, there is a distinct lick of brass to the air which today is discreetly lacking.

A lovely job in a theatre! An ice rink in the square at night! Why should I be denied these things? (It is because I do not deserve them).

The wolf, staying now for the duration of winter, is capricious: 'I can't stand you any longer!' he hollers. Moments later he's taken me to town to buy me all of Chuck Palahniuk's novels. 'These are really good,' he says. 'You'll love this guy.'

My girlfriend and I agree that the wolf should pursue a career—and there is just the position for him at Whitehall:

WOLF REQUIRED, £20 per hour.

The wolf applies, commutes to his interview and, two days hence, is informed through the mail that, even in the face of gross competition, he has been given the post.

'Yipee!' he says—and sets off for Whitehall.

'So what does the job involve?' I ask, that night.

'Nothing,' says the wolf. 'As I understand it, they mean to pay me simply for being a wolf.'

IV

The Wolf and Religion: The wolf is Presbyterian.

'I don't know an awful lot about Calvinism,' he says, 'but as I see it, I'm *predestined* not to. I leave that sort of thing to the Lay Elders.'

'Does the Presbyterian church even *exist* anymore?' I ask. 'I thought they came up with it on a boat and it lasted the duration of the crossing.'

'No, that's Lutherism: after which he translated the bible into German, but was excommunicated by the Diet of Worms . . .'

'What's the Diet of Worms?'

'I don't know. Something to do with eating worms.'

'I'd look it up, but we used the encyclopaedia to make that raft last summer.'

'Yeah,' says the Wolf, 'that was a great Summer.'

~

The Wolf and his ailments: A progressively diminishing ability of the eye to focus.

My girlfriend takes milk and water down to the employees of the arboretum. As a symptom of dehydration and sleep-deprivation many of them now believe that they are Hydra—and challenge passers-by to lop off a head.

'Boy,' says the Wolf, leaning over my shoulder, 'you're like living proof that a little knowledge is a dangerous thing.'

V

Today the wolf is throwing sweets at me, scattershots of Dollymixture and chocolate covered peanuts.

'Look at this!' he says, furious. 'Press clippings from the future!'

He produces some yellowed scraps of paper:

> *'The characterisation of the Wolf is brilliant. You can almost feel his breath on the back of your neck.'—The Tribune*

I feel the wolf's hot breath on the back of my neck.

'Read the next one.'

> *'I really like the bit where the wolf goes to prison.'—James, age 6*

'What's that about?' he demands. 'Am I going to prison?'

'These look more like press-clippings from the *past*,' I say. 'Probably a review of some other book about a wolf.'

The wolf is crestfallen. He coughs, he sits on his haunches. He stands up again.

'There are *other* wolves?'

'Not for me,' I pat him on the head, but it seems to grant scant comfort.

Log Cabin

I

It is always a surprise to see wolverines pouring over the mountain. Even when it happens each morning at exactly the same time. In the snow my coffee cup billows like a stage-prop cauldron and I have wrapped the fish in the snow for tomorrow.

I'm so glad I can't speak your language. And that I am no longer proud—even of not being proud. Before you left for work you said, 'There are things about myself I don't want to know; there just are; I just don't.' You were still asleep as you caught the skiff to main-street.

Convalescing since I tore that hamstring, I've been whittling a mountain range out of a giant block of Kendal Mint Cake. It's a—what's the word?—a *microcosm*, right? You really can't smoke up here. I'm reading *The Raspberry Paradox*. It's overrated.

However, there is butter in the butter churn. The furnace glares. Even in conversation you evoke the entire scene and all the people in a single word: *hungry*, say, or *crepuscular*—and that's why I love you. On the shelf sit two unopened letters, both hand addressed. This may sound naïve, but everything is just going to get better and better forever.

II

One of them was carrying a parasol. I think they were headed to the beach—which is hundreds of miles away. I followed them, ducking behind mounds of snow that I might eavesdrop.

'... but I think if you start complaining about hypocrisy, you just end up sounding like a whiner. The point is merely not to be false. Criticising anyone is overcompensation. Don't tell people how you're living your life; live your life. If it's any good they may follow you ...'

'I think you are drafted, like one of Nietzsche's identikit pilgrims, lousily on purpose, to give the argument against being a pilgrim more clout,' said the girl with the parasol.

When I grew tired of listening and emerged from the snow, I met a mimetic fellow on the other side of the path who had been prying on the same conversation.

'Did you *hear* them?' I said, eyes wide with awe.

'I know,' he said. 'Stuck up little bitches. And what's with that stupid parasol?'

At home I boil the kettle and read one of the letters.

> *Now the artist and the philistine must both throw rocks at the city walls. You think there is hope but you're wrong.*

It's cold and the record player requires a new needle—not that I'm crazy about Dean Martin anyway. By the time you return from the commissary I have singularly failed to build a fire.

III

You: asleep in the furs. It will take a decade's practice before I even *try* to describe you.

'Ha ha,' I say, taking the air, beating the rug and clearing the snow-drift from the door. The commissary has closed for stock-count. It is your day off.

A letter has arrived:

You'd better make sure we don't get bored today!

Which strikes me as wonderful advice, if indelicately put. What emotional light! Even your nasty collection of perpetual motion dolls cannot upset me.

'Coffee?' you say, opening your eyes.

There is business to attend to, old grounds to be thrown away. Time is plastic: each duty can be encouraged to swell up and fill the morning. How I love to wash the dishes and listen to the news. Even really, really bad news.

At the window I count to three.

'It wasn't a dream,' you murmur and roll onto your side. 'That stone will grant you less pleasure and kindle more desire every time you look at it.'

Awash in the tide of wolverines I notice a peach and turquoise parasol.

IV

The five perpetual motion dolls are finely crafted and calibrated with tiny internal weights so as to never stop moving. One: a fisherman in a big yellow mac. He is a stubbly, glaring man with a pipe in his mouth. He nods, constantly. The worst: a clown in a metallic purple jump-suit. He juggles a chrome-plated crucifix from hand to hand. I don't even want to go into the other three right now. I arrived home one night and they were there on the shelf and you said, 'Do you like them?'

In the evening we attend the Agnostic Temple. I on crutches. During the silences we are encouraged to worry about our MasterCard repayments and how our hair looks. The minister is using his fax machine analogy again.

'Each time the message is reiterated, the content is distorted further until it eventually becomes exactly the opposite message. Or, at least, a message so vague as to be ripe for interpretation by one with an ulterior motive. Let us, therefore, take great pains to create an entirely new message each time; never to repeat a fragment or a sentiment. In the name of whatever inchoate force may or may not exist–'

Amen. On the way home I slip over and land on my back. People in dark coats brush over me, apologising. The stars! How could I have failed to mention the stars?

While I heat the goulash you pace, worrying, and lay out the work clothes because you have to work tomorrow. Soon, in the oil lamp's native glow, you have gone to sleep.

'You're happy here, aren't you?' I say.

The fisherman leers.

V

This morning an ill fitting shirt gets stuck on my head. By the time I've pulled it over my face, you are gone. The cabin shakes under an aeroplane. I don't often realise how one thing effects another—and the days pass like little sailors, tapping at the window, trying to regale me with their boring nightmares.

A perpetual motion doll—the Lieutenant—falls from the shelf and smashes. I rake up the pieces, pausing to note that, far from containing tiny weights and pulleys, the doll is hollow. I boil water for coffee, but the tin is empty. I turn off the stove and watch the desperately clear water simmer down, take a walk.

Objects are difficult to look at today—the snow; the damp tassels of the fir tree; a rusted wheel-barrow on one elbow like Charlie Brown. I rest on the crutches, watching plumes of breath.

I think I will ask you to leave the log cabin, although you will cry, and I will cry and we won't want to leave each other.

A letter informs me:

> *They have taken to the streets, committing all sorts of enormities. We cried and they said, 'Stop crying.'*
>
> *Maybe you could come and impersonate us for a while, take the heat off? It is all very well to argue about solipsism, but what about the likes of us who don't know what the word solipsism means?*

The piano tuner arrives to tune the piano. I don't have a piano.

VI

Tonight a storm erupts over the city. Nightmares have preludes: I put the remaining perpetual motion dolls in a sack and leave it outside the door.

The material world is progressing endlessly in a series of cycles. I heat a tin of Black and White soup over the stove and pour a bowl for you—although it's obvious you're staying at the commissary, which is where I bought the tin of Black and White soup, three years ago. ('Oh, you like Black and White soup, too?' you said. 'I love the way it's chequered.')

This is what prevents me from taking a swim in the black lake: not a fear of drowning or freezing to death (one of which fates would almost certainly befall me), but rather that I have grown accustomed to never swimming in the black lake at night; irrational, talismanic fear. It is important not to give yourself too much credit.

I undo the clasp on a leather book under your side of the bed, but your last diary entry is encrypted—and that's a little too cute, a little too appropriate. I am forever writing in the margins of my life.

A knock at the door. In my rush to open it I spill the tinned pineapples onto my sock.

A figure in a great coat, swaddled in a thick scarf and a woollen hat stands in the doorway—although that sort of goes without saying in a blizzard, doesn't it?

'Steve?' I say.

VII

'Liar, liar, lie,' sings Steve, in a sweet falsetto. Steve is my half-brother; an artist from the city.

'I'm going to have to stay here a while,' says Steve, picking a cross-section of pineapple from the floor and dropping it into his mouth. 'The city is a theatre of cruelty. You're going to have a lot of people hiding-out here—that's my guess—and they'll be wounded and bereaved and probably quite depressing, so you'd better get used to the idea.'

I make up the camp-bed, Steve still singing, 'Liar, liar, lie,' as he takes off his coat and rolls his scarf into a ball.

'Nicola left you or something?'

'She's at the commissary.'

'Oh dear,' says Steve.

I go to bed with a glass of Napoleon brandy and Steve's present—a dirty, grey feather, which I stick to the wall with a piece of blu-tac.

~

Morning and the frost encroaches halfway across the cabin. I awake to a market-stall commotion and find a family of six sitting around my table. Steve entertains them with a tin whistle and they are all singing, 'Liar, liar, lie.'

VIII

Equilibrium is the terrifying state all nature tends towards. The wolverines go pouring over the mountain like mercury.

A letter arrives:

> *It seems you have mistaken your understanding of the world for the world itself.*
>
> *It is embarrassing to watch you brandishing that which we hold to be self-evident like a child with a new word.*

Steve and the itinerant family are playing pinochle with a short deck. I'm putting on several coats. The father shakes his head and widens his eyes.

'Sit with us and play a hand or two,' says Steve, flatly, pulling out an orange crate.

'But I can't hold the cards in these gloves,' I say, turning to the door.

EPILOGUE

'Well, I'm not crazy about this town either,' you said, folding the hamburger meat in the grease-proof paper. 'We could have a miserable life together.'

'I'd like that,' I said. I put the last tin of Black and White soup in my rucksack and hoisted it onto my back.

'Seventeen pounds and twenty-seven pence,' you said.

'Don't be fooled by the romantic invalid-loner shtick,' I said, handing you a twenty. 'I'm as boring and feckless as the next man.'

'What's it like, up on the mountain?' you said.

'Cold,' I said. 'And there are wolverines every day. And I keep getting these stupid letters.'

The floor of the commissary was compacted dirt, and God's love, here symbolised by fluorescent strip lighting, shone down upon it.

'You must be up there for some reason,' you said, tucking a lock of hair behind your ear.

'Reason dissipates with altitude,' I said. 'I suppose I just like mountains.'

Scarecrow

I kissed the scarecrow: the scarecrow was cold and inert and tasted of sawdust. It was damn silly. Abelard took the photographs and advised me as to how I should kiss the scarecrow—with a hand on its shoulder, for instance.

After the shoot I purchased an *Avian Guide* from an unmanned stall, placing a note in a rusty can. The guide began:

> *Every bird that flits across our path contains a pea-sized brain which the bird uses for navigation, muscle control, detection of predators and tweeting.*

On its way to my pocket a ten pence piece glinted in the moonlight. I checked the date (1992) and the tiny but unmissable chink one micron to the left of the Queen's earring. This very coin had turned up in my change during most—if not all—moments of significance in my life to date.

I went to sit by the river to reflect on what its arrival might portend on this occasion, but was immediately seized, bound hand and foot and carried into town. 'Like scarecrows, do you?' said the grubby-faced men.

During my trial the judge's contact microphone kept losing power. 'Foul . . . Unnatural . . . Halcyon . . . Porous . . .' he said.

Next day they attached me to a post in the middle of an oceanic cornfield and left me for dead. A crow landed on my shoulder and whispered, 'You do realise, old thing, that we're not actually the *least* bit scared of you?'

The Wolf's Career

I

THE WOLF AS CLERGYMAN

'Because I was the youngest among seven brothers,' declares the wolf, 'it is only fitting that I become a school-master or a member of the clergy.'

I tell the wolf that the socio-economic structure of the country has changed a lot in the last three centuries—but he calls me a chalk-eater and a crummy, one-eyed lush.

Later that week he is ordained by the Lutheran church and I arrive late on my bicycle to hear his inaugural sermon. The church is full of tiny yellow flowers. The wolf struts around the podium.

'For is it not so that true knowledge is impossible? And is it not equally so that if true knowledge *were* possible, it would corrupt even the most virtuous through pride, hegemony and elitism. Therefore let us be ugly and stupid on purpose. For that which is already corrupt can no more be corrupted than a man who swims underwater can be drenched by the rain.'

The wolf leads the congregation in reciting the Wolf's Prayer:

> *When I am without sin,*
> *Let me cast the first stone,*
> *And when I am without pride,*
> *Let them build a statue in my honour.*

Later that week he is excommunicated for advocating a peasant's revolt and leaves, muttering, 'Call themselves revisionist.'

II

THE WOLF AS MEMOIRIST

I abandoned the boat in the shallows and swam to shore, my knees beating against the world.

'That seems awfully arrogant,' I tell the wolf. 'It implies that you regard the world as your drum.'

'Nonsense,' says the wolf, scratching behind his ears. 'I regard the world as my donkey.'

'That's rather arrogant, too,' I say. 'And if you want my opinion, I'd cut the slanderous comments about Free Masons and Scientologists that make up the last half of the book—neither tribe takes kindly to criticism.'

Annabelle starts playing her cello next door. The wolf drops his bottle of ink and turns on me.

'You,' he says, 'are a *slow puncture*—for nobody knows how leaky you are until you are tested and all your virtues are revealed chimerical. If nothing is done about you, you will become flaccid and bring down all those relying upon you. Your every word is like a bone in a pie and I shall devote a whole book of my memoir to lambasting you.'

III

THE WOLF AS EDUCATOR

The walls of the classroom are covered in paintings and dry-pasta collages of the wolf.

'It's brilliant,' he tells me. 'These noble, bloodthirsty creatures are far better than you. *Par example*, if one weak child has a toy that another, stronger child wants, the stronger child will take the toy. I see no such bravery in you—for you are as a flannel used to sop milk from the breakfast bar.'

One morning he invites me to read his pupils a story, but then quite forgets he has invited me and I am left loitering in the foyer as he holds forth.

'I see you children as a wild thought plantation,' the wolf informs his class. 'It is not for me to tell you what one-in-six of you will die of—nor even the more pressing matter of what one-in-*three* of you will die of. No. I am here to bid you live.'

The wolf reads to the class from a book of his own stories:

> 'There was once a wolf—who owned many beautiful cars and a handsome, admirable tail—who sat next to a miserable man on a bus.
>
> "What have you got to look so pleased about?" said the miserable man.
>
> Reader, I ate him.'

IV

THE WOLF AS CHEF

If you order duck in the wolf's restaurant, the wolf brings you a bronze statue of a duck on a white plate and watches as you try to eat it.

'More sauce with your bronze duck?' he will say.

Nevertheless, he is a garrulous host. Should you comment that the light is effulgent this evening, he will slap you on the back, saying:

'Yes. It reminds me of Goethe's last words: "Open the second shutter so more light can come in." An epigram so understated one hardly notices it—like a thumb-tack on a chair. But, when one pauses to reflect, it is not only wholly appropriate, but quite poignant—like a thumb-tack in the buttock.'

And then he will make quite some exhibition in opening the second shutter so more light can come in.

V

THE WOLF AS MERCHANT SEAMAN

'All vessels lost!' wails the wolf. 'Spices, razor wire, candy hearts, underwear—not to mention a thousand poor sailors' wives deprived of their sailors. And all because you lit your cigarette from a candle! Truly you are the B-Side to an insipid song. Ten months at sea, each one an unmitigated disaster!'

The wolf remains apoplectic until I agree to take him to the pub.

As we stumble home along the cliff at dusk, the wolf becomes wistful, leaning towards me.

'I can see the ship I should have left on reflected in your eye as it disappears over the horizon, each porthole a tiny disc of light gliding over your iris and into your tear duct,' he says. 'And as the wind flattens the wild grass and disorders your hair, I am clasped by the desire to throw you into the sea. But I'll not do it, much as every cell of my being compels me otherwise. You just remember that.'

A buzzard spreads its wings and goes without saying over the precipice.

VI

THE WOLF AS PLAYWRIGHT

'Don't think it's escaped my attention,' I tell the wolf, 'that all of your plays contain lecterns.'

'What's that supposed to mean?' snaps the wolf, taking off his spectacles.

'That, freed from responsibility or fear of reprisal, you are using your characters to voice some of your less agreeable opinions.'

'If not caring about people and eating them is disagreeable, then so be it,' says the wolf. 'I'm neither physician nor philosopher. I merely diagnose a terrible crapulence, have the fortune teller set fire to the executive's house and conclude on some joyless chit about how lucky we all are. It's called having a social conscience. Now if you wouldn't mind making yourself scarce, I've invited some friends from the cast round to tea. They're decent, plain-spoken sorts and they wouldn't like you.'

I take my newspaper to the park and sit on a commemorative bench. A girl in a black dress-suit tries to sell me a toaster. There is an amber note of despair in her face—so I buy the toaster and carry it around with me for the rest of the evening.

VII

THE WOLF AS LIEUTENANT

A dark shape creeps along the windowsill. It is the peak of the wolf's cap and the wolf, marching.

'Indeed,' he says, 'deceit no longer offends me. I fight because I believe that my enemy has been deceived by an evil man and that my ally has been deceived by a good man.'

The wolf is posted abroad and I don't hear from him for several years.

One Tuesday in July Annabelle receives a postcard. It is addressed to Annabelle and begins *Dear Annabelle.*

> *It was lovely of you to put me up for such a long time. I am sorry if I inconvenienced you in any way.*
>
> *At times of great sorrow I hear the camber of your cello and it reminds me that mankind reached its zenith with the invention of the cello and has been going downhill ever since.*
>
> *Yours,*
>
> *Wolf*
> *x*

'Odd that he doesn't even mention you,' says Annabelle, placing the postcard under the clock.

'I don't know,' I say. 'Maybe he thinks I'm the answer to the riddle.'

Which, now that I think about it, is hardly a compliment.

The Esplanade

I

In the esplanade everyone is trying to act natural.

A spy named *Red Fox and His Canoe* is having a frightful argument with his wife.

A visitor sits at a chess table with his type-writer. A writer sits at the adjacent table smoking a cigarillo. A travel-writer plays a Spanish guitar and drinks from a chipped glass of vodka. He pauses to make a note of how nice that is.

Sitting in the esplanade with a Spanish guitar drinking vodka from a chipped glass is damnably pleasant.

The writer sighs and draws on his cigarillo. A woman in national costume passes and they stare at her.

Poor fool thinks he's broadening everyone's horizons, deems the writer, tapping ash on his shoes, *when really he's like a tourist buying a phial of famous dirt.*

The travel-writer looks over his shoulder. *The English are such wasteful clinicians*, he notes in the dog-eared notepad, *irritable, but not passionate*. He cuts his lip on the chipped glass.

On the casino wall someone has written *DEATH TO ALL EXTREMISTS*, under which a pedagogic hand has added *INCLUDING YOU SWEETIE*.

I sit on the shoe shop, watching it all through a tin rifle-sight.

II

Red Fox and His Canoe buys a crème de menthe and orders the calamari. His wife sings 'When I Fall In Love' and receives a standing ovation from everyone in the esplanade except *Red Fox and His Canoe* who reads, in the newspaper, a bad review of the restaurant he is sitting in.

His wife wears an alabaster dress and a porcelain orchid in her hair. She isn't really his wife.

The travel-writer searches for interesting people to implement. The writer glares at him from the chess tables. The visitor yawns and begins to type. A boy stands at his side and asks him what he's writing and goes through his pockets, making off with a black leather folio wallet and a cigar.

I have a clear shot on *Red Fox and His Canoe*—and can imagine the baroque unfurling of his death: an Eastern European flag against a white sky—and he would relish it as much as I. But it is fitting to let him live a little longer.

A scuffle breaks between the writer and the travel-writer. They roll over one another in the dust and the travel-writer gets in a few good punches before Maria breaks them up. Last night she found her way into my dreams again.

The trap-door scrapes and my shoulders tense—but it is only Jorge with more wine and a quilt.

'Thanks, Jorge.'

'You take it easy up here,' advises Jorge. 'It's set to be a cold night.'

III

A butler walks through the esplanade, beating the ground with a switch. '. . . And what if I *do* want discourse of reason?' he mutters. 'What if I *do*?' His hands are exquisitely manicured; tiny white jewels set in the cuticles. That briefcase looks heavy.

Everything is orange and blue in the twilight. I eat a raw quail's egg, swallowing it whole and using the constricting muscles of my throat to break the shell. It's an old snake trick I learned from TV.

A well-thumbed photocopied essay entitled: 'A Fragmentary History of *Red Fox and His Canoe* and Why He is Considered a Threat' lies by my shoe, annotated with yellow high-lighter and carmine splotches of wine.

> 1.1 *Red Fox and His Canoe* reflects on his late teens, working in a second-hand bookshop: 'Back then all I cared about was whether people had the correct change. Sometimes—when they didn't have the correct change—I'd slip a fire-ant into their bag along with the books they'd bought. And on occasion, I am convinced, the fire-ant would later bite them.' [*Chuckles softly*.]

The writer sits by the broken fountain, dabbing his mouth with a napkin. In his notebook he has written,

> *I'll hawk him like a watch. Like a watch.*

A little yellow bird lands by his side and bursts into song / flames.

IV

The butler walks right over to *Red Fox and His Canoe*'s table. He places the briefcase in front of *Red Fox and His Canoe*'s counterfeit wife. She shakes her head, but the butler pops the catches and the briefcase opens. Whatever happens next is obscured by stage mist.

The travel-writer and the writer are playing a game of chess with Maria's old set. They have replaced the nine missing pawns with empty beer bottles. In the middle of a particularly well cultivated attack on the part of the writer, a passing concierge sweeps the empty bottles onto his tray and swerves back into the kitchen.

'You want one of these pies?' says Jorge, appearing from the trap-door with a baking-tray.

'I don't know.' I look up from my rifle sight. 'What's in them?'

Jorge frowns at the horizon for a while.

'Little porcelain ballerinas,' he says.

The stage mist begins to dissipate. *Red Fox and His Canoe* sits at his table, toying with a butterknife. The butler has vanished with his wife.

I tell Jorge that's pretty funny, but when I bite into one of the pies I scrape the roof of my mouth on a tiny pointed foot.

V

Red Fox and His Canoe now sits like a vice with his forehead on the table. From this I infer that he has failed in a matter of some significance.

During the war they sent a little bi-plane over the esplanade towing a banner that read:

EVERYONE YOU LOVE IS DEAD

in eight languages. I'm about to squeeze the trigger when the bell announces midnight and Adrian puts a cold, heavy hand on my shoulder. 'Time to clock-off, kid,' he growls.

Jorge sits at his desk holding three black nails between his lips and tapping the sole of a bright green shoe with a miniature hammer.

'I don't trust that Adrian guy,' he mumbles. 'He smells funny and one of his hands is made of black glass. When I was a boy you wouldn't trust a man like that, but these days they give him a gun and let him sit on top of my shop.' He brushes down the green espadrilles and hands them to me. I buckle them to my feet.

It is a pithy, mesmerising night.

VI

The governor takes a seat at the table of *Red Fox and His Canoe* and pours a glass of Retsina into his mouth. He tells a joke.

'What could drive a man to casually toss a grenade like he's delivering a newspaper?' he says. 'Depressingly little.'

'If history has taught us anything,' agrees *Red Fox and His Canoe*, 'which it almost certainly has not, it is this.'

The chef bashes pots and pans, but when the kitchen door is finally unlocked, not a single utensil has been sullied.

Seems like Jorge was right not to trust Adrian—for no sooner have I sat down at an adjacent table and opened up my newspaper than he opens fire on everyone in the restaurant. He also shoots: a well-dressed couple emerging from the casino, the writer and the travel-writer at their chess table, a bottle of vermouth behind the bar and a sand-coloured dog who had been chewing its paw under the rubber tree, scrunching his nose up like a disapproving child and chewing that paw as if his life depended on it, which, as it transpires, I suppose it did.

'. . . with the unstudied vehemence of a cynic discovering an ethos . . .' says *Red Fox and His Canoe*, dying.

'It has always bothered me that soldiers call us "civilians" without suppressing the superior timbre in their voices,' confesses the governor, dying.

VII

'Hey buddy,' says Adrian, purveyor of loins, purloiner of veils, 'we won!'

He puts a heavy glass arm around my shoulder. I can see the stars reflected in it.

'Geeze, Adrian,' I say, shaking him off, 'did you have to kill that dog and all those people? If you're trying to make a point about the dehumanising influence of espionage, it's a really heavy-handed one.'

'Pah,' says Adrian, spitting out a pinch of chewing tobacco. 'God's the one allowing us to suffer.'

I know I will likely live to regret it, but I can think of no course of action other than to damn Adrian, there and then, standing in the ashes and sand, standing under the stars in the esplanade, damn him. And, thusly damned, Adrian's glass arm begins to give out blinding flashes of light and he drops to his knees, howling.

'You could do worse than commit this to memory,' I tell him.

VIII

In the walled garden I keep in lieu of a house, I notice a devil watching me from the liquidambar tree. It sniggers, falls out of the tree and scuttles back up the branches again, hoping I haven't noticed. I'm not sure how it figures that—as its head is an inverted cone sucking in light and its tail is longer than an architectural frieze, depicting the struggles of my people up to the present day.

Arranged sequentially on the devil's tail like that, they don't amount to much. As peoples go, one might even call us fortunate.

I lie in the middle of the lawn throwing a rubber ball into the air and catching it. Sometimes I miss and the rubber ball bounces off my chest and into the phlox, followed by protracted searching.

I am not tied to the rubber ball, but an observer would be forgiven.

Soon, while scrabbling in the phlox, my hand alights on a tusk. It is another devil, hiding among the flowers. (I knew I shouldn't have damned Adrian). This one has tiny silver county councillors for eyes.

'It's a fine thing to talk of ethics and principles when most people just choke on their pen-lids,' it splutters. 'Don't try to argue with me. I've seen the X-rays.'

How easy to suggest that all is meaningless, to suggest it again and again.

EPILOGUE

'Which reminds me,' says the butler, next morning, pouring tea for me and Emily, the widow of *Red Fox and His Canoe*, 'Recently I was unable to rebuke thoughts of pride, lust and avarice and now they have taken root in my inmost being. I return to them as I would to a place of rest or a lover's arms.' The sunlight catches his cuticle diamonds.

'That's what you get for working in television,' says Emily, taking a handful of fresh mint leaves from the bush and shredding them into my teacup before pouring the hot tea over my head. 'But you don't have to like what you're fed. My advice is to scrape by on your own native intelligence.'

A starchy voice on the radio announces we are at war.

If you answered mostly STRONGLY DISAGREE, you are a freedom fighter.

The devils twitter and coruscate. I could dismiss them, all the devils, as residual phenomena, only Emily *will* keep arguing with them. 'If you have ever bullied or gossiped about somebody, you aren't worth dying for,' she says.

Sometimes the devils are prevalent as rain—and you can barely see the sky for all the brightly coloured sepulchres falling out of their mouths.

Hair-pullers and clothes-horses, obeying orders.

The rest of my days in quiet refutation. The rest of my days in quiet refutation. The rest of my days in quiet refutation.

Notes

The Solex Brothers

I.

'Solex' means the energy from the sun (*Journal of Solar Studies*, WINTER, Vol. 23, Issue 12: 1981). I distinctly recall Peter Mandelson saying something about politics being 'in his hair' in Durham when he was accidentally re-elected as part of the general election in the year 2000 or whenever it was. And the electorate of Durham looked on in dismay, even though they were the ones who'd voted him in again, perhaps having forgotten that he was Peter Mandelson. And then he screamed 'I HAVE THE STEEL IN ME!' seven or eight times and danced a horrid little jig, which will be burned onto the retinas of my generation (who were, at the time, studying for degrees and staying up late drinking cheap cider and eating chocolate lollies in the shape of the party leaders) forever. So the politician in question here is Mandelson.

The tiny blue birds are supposed to look like an early Disney film; an animated swallow motif fluttering around the live-action train. Twice the size of ordinary men is actually pretty big, isn't it? I should have said half-again. Hmm. In *Frank* (1995), Jim Woodring's hallucinatory comic strip about a blue cat, people are always getting their heads stuck in things with the most horrible consequences. This motif informs much of my work and, indeed, much of my life—constant nightmares about getting stuck in tiny windows and doors.

The simple inversion of a cliché 'Oh cruel fate!', is obvious enough, right? Our narrator is not unlike Charles Baudelaire's *flâneur*, a morbidly disengaged figure, unable to halt the inexorable course of his own life or comprehend the reasons behind his own choices—a state neatly reflected by the unalterable course of a train. This is kind of a 'prose poetry in-joke'. How annoying of me. Anyway, this page has hopefully set the milieu—trains with compartments, little cucumber sandwiches, bowler hats. And the narrator is sort of me and sort of the narrator of a fairy-tale.

II.

The sandwich board reads: SANDWICHES—SOLD OUT

I think the song speaks for itself. It's not based on anything. It's just a harmless chauffeur song. But anyway: a field of inedible vegetables is a complete waste of time, unless you're going to make them into little sculptures by putting cartoon eyes on them. 'Midden' is the territorial excrement left by a kind of seabird or mollusc. So a 'midden boy' would be any young man who, metaphorically or otherwise, feels the need to assert himself and defend whatever he believes through foul, odious acts and statements. Songs anti- and pro- *really do* have dead melodies—in so far as they compromise their beauty and their ridiculous, unquestionable right to exist in favour of some kind of (usually pretty obvious and redundant) agenda and thereby pervert and kill it. 'For tuppence I'll show you my scar' is not only a good example of such a song but a side-swipe at overly confessional poetry (if that seems mean-spirited, I'd like to add that overly confessional poetry started it by accusing me of failing to 'reveal enough of myself within my work.'). Gosh, this is even better than I thought it was. What a clever little man I am. It is also a reference to the Disney film *Mary Poppins* (1862) in which TUPPENCE is something of a metonym for a father's love for his children; a metonym which is modulated to several different causes and eventually restored in an act of absolute narrative genius. It is the cost of feeding the birds ('tuppence a bag'), the value that we are encouraged to invest in the bank and, finally, the price of paper and string. It is also the cost of Burt's flatcap.

The modulation has always fascinated me—and it's been a mainstay of the prose poem since Gertrude Stein, I shouldn't wonder. So the meanings here are somewhat secondary to the manner in which the lines are phonetically similar to the first verse. I have more verses somewhere. In the Coen brothers' *O Brother, Where Art Thou?*, the politician on his carnival float is always talking about 'the Little Guy', as in the small business owner.

If you don't get the diner/bookshelf analogy, it's probably because you HATE BOOKS.

III.

Lucida is the name of a font. This is probably the least inspired example of character naming since Dalwood Brokenn's *Next Time I'll Kill You* in which the detective protagonist is called Times Newroman.

IV.

Between third and fourth stanzas the Solex Brothers have become my tutors and their library is full of empty books and I'm supposed to listen to them hold forth and approve of their ridiculous gestures, many of which seem designed specifically to annoy me, butterflies notwithstanding. This is probably more subconscious carping about poetry. '. . . *whether caked in silence or snagged on promise*' is the kind of flowery nonsense that initially appears to make a kind of coherent sense, albeit operating under its own logic: it's easy to imagine something caked in silence, just like a key in a cake is caked in a cake. However, being snagged on promise is vaguer—promise as in potential; snagged as in tearing a shirt on a badly made chicken wire fence (probably shouldn't have been crawling under it anyway) —presumably referring to the disastrous ramifications of unfulfilled potential and punning on promise (as in having sworn to fulfil your potential) and now having to face the consequences, the snag—grabbed by the elbow, say—being only the beginning. 'What have you done to your kite?' the inevitable follow-up. Note that these kites exist not only within people, but within all things in the transfigured world. I suppose, seeing as this is something the Solex Brothers are teaching me, it is appropriate that it makes only dubious sense.

'*I soon swore off . . . fragments of mistrust.*' This time taking a sideswipe at the polar opposite to overly confessional poetry: fragmentary experimental stuff. Parataxis is 'the juxtaposition of clauses without the use of a conjunction.' So it all comes out sounding like a badly translated crossword puzzle. And for what? To let us know that language and meaning are fragile or long-dead or whatever. SNORE! Hence the 'fragments of mistrust'—as the only thing this kind of poetry communicates is a vague, grumpy disaffection with consumerism or something else the poet is pissed off about but won't tell us exactly what it is—but hey, it seems to sell a few books to equally vaguely pissed off people who like turning their barely-formed ennui into an art-form. I just hope they use recycled paper and aren't, say, employed by a state / free-market funded institution like a university is all, otherwise it feels a bit hypocritical.

V.

The Solex Brothers live as if life were a Japanese illustration—and in this stanza the narrator realises that he is merely a strand of creeping ivy in their frieze.

VI.

Here we learn, albeit obliquely, that the Solex Brothers have offended everyone in the vicinity. For instance it is revealed that the chauffeur's song from chapter II contained barbs against, among other people, an innocent arable farmer. So I guess it wasn't so harmless after all.

I once lodged on a street that had its own hall—in the manner of a town or village hall, but solely for that street. There was a noticeboard which was not, to my disappointment, full of scurrilous gossip about (and by) the fifty or so occupants of the Victorian terraces, but rather held general announcements about dog fouling and a proposal for a new footpath to the high street.

VII.

More so than any other poem in this book, 'The Solex Brothers' makes use of collage and mishearings from the radio, TV, etc. The Brother's statements, once they are robbed of sense, all come from things that I picked up from my dad's bookshelves. *The Snow People* is the title of a history of Lapland, I think. Who says I'm not an experimental poet? Oh. Experimental poets. (*Sobs.*)

VIII.

The Solex Brothers' speech: 'What would you become outside my mansion, outside this vessel? It might pay you in time and health. It seems almost unnaturally warm. I got in with him and said, "Eight!" And instantly his whole notion of the outer world becomes a blank! The idea of Good Work is not quite extinct among us: my thighs are huge and so is my belly. Queeny shrieked as the pan of livers clattered to the kitchen floor.'

'I have always been fond of tracing to its source in nature any prevailing custom. In between the buzzes a distant baritone voice can be heard: 'So is it okay if Kate and her friends come?' Do you wish to know what happened? I exerted all my powers to make her misjudgement plausible. We must, every one of us, choose between friendship and indifference.'

[*Fanfare. Blackout.*]

EPILOGUE

For the record, I think this is really bad advice.

To a Wolf

I.

Screaming 'Whoooo!' is one of those stupid personal references; a friend of mine had a nightmare in which he was being followed through some dingy twilight streets by someone or something—he never saw them, but was keenly aware of being stared at. Then he saw a face in a darkened window and promptly woke up screaming 'Whooo! Whooo!' It took his girlfriend half an hour to calm him down. I've always found that sort of funny—you know, other people's psychological trauma. So anyway, in this case I'm obviously screaming 'who?' as in, who would do such a thing? What's going on with the capital letters here?

The wolf's show—to which nobody turns up—is probably my subconscious disappointment about pretty much everything I've ever done. Did I say subconscious? I meant *conscious*. The 'something else' refers to an act of callousness and self-involvement the narrator perpetrated in 1997 which is none of your damn business.

II.

An arboretum being a sort of nursery for the cultivation of trees and shrubs. In this case I had in mind a kind of giant greenhouse, open to the public. With concierges, like a hotel. How exactly can *moss* be scathing? What on Earth was I talking about? The arboretum functions as a distraction from the wolf—just a location in the narrator's town—and the venue for the wolf's show. Arboretums also feature in Lucy Clan na Gael's Celtic mystery, *The Pedagogue*—about a disaffected maths teacher who is also a murderer. He kills his victims using Euclid's Parallel Axiom.

References to the narrator's own story about a wolf form the meta-narrative of 'To a Wolf'. The only reason the wolf is hanging around is because he thinks he's going to star in a novel—unaware that the narrator is, at the most, a minor talent. However, in the last sentence the wolf seems to be referring to the very prose poem as it unfolds—and is dissatisfied by how circumlocutory it is—a customary trait of the kind of smart-arse thing I tend to write. Hence he cites a couple of pleasant wolf metaphors as might appear in a *proper* poem about a wolf. This is how you have your cake and eat it. Or, at least, it would be if anybody was paying any attention to your work in the first place.

III.

I lost nights of sleep trying to work out whether I wanted to say '*discretely*' or '*discreetly* lacking'. I think I was reading a book about English usage at the time. Anyway, I settled for 'discrete' to mean distinctly—thinking it would mean *definitely, absolutely*. Which is not the kind of 'distinct' the word 'discrete' refers to at all; that being *separate, individually delineated*, like an aeroplane meal. In retrospect, 'discreetly lacking', meaning subtly, unobtrusively lacking would have been the better choice. So I've restored that for this edition.

IV.

I'm not sure what kind of a beef I had with Calvinism when I wrote this. I guess it was Calvin's ridiculous concept of Original Sin which almost put paid to Christianity altogether. Anyway, it gets all mixed up with the Lutheran and Presbyterian church here—in a sort of *White Noise* half-deliberate half- true stupidity and ignorance on my part. The Diet of Worms was the council at which Luther was excommunicated. This chapter could also be taken as a parody of poetry's obsession with historical detail—the more obscure and inexplicable the better. This, as far as I'm concerned, is a wrong turning as a result of completely missing the fact that T. S. Eliot was *joking*. At least until *Four Quartets*. Oh, and like II, it also ends in self-reflexivity—as if the wolf is reading the poem in real-time, as it is written.

V.

I don't know why I expected this to make sense. A wolf wouldn't have a very complete working understanding of time—therefore to him, if a press clipping could come from the past and arrive in the present for discussion, why not the future?

ADVERTISEMENT

James, age 6, reappears in 'Wolf in Commerce' from *The Harbour Beyond the Movie* and in further, forthcoming Wolf adventures.

Log Cabin

I.

A man lives in a log cabin on the side of a snowy mountain. He once lived there as a hermit, but his girlfriend, Nicola, has recently moved in with him. They live simply and happily, worrying only about cooking and eating. The city beneath the mountain has been torn by civil war for years—even the supermarket where Nicola works is called the commissary—but the situation has recently degenerated into outright violence between those who perpetrate atrocities but only because atrocities have been perpetrated against them (the TWPABOBAPAT) and those who have had atrocities perpetrated against them and therefore commit atrocities in retaliation (the TWAPATTCAR). The national religion: agnosticism.

Given that he has sworn off media of any kind, the narrator receives news solely through hand-written letters (probably from his half brother, Steve)—which are mostly riddles without answers, menacing but nonsensical.

I was going to use a different made-up rhetorical device in each piece, but in the end it wasn't working out. However, the ruins of my intentions are sometimes more visible than others. This one is full of oxymorons and contradictions of the basest, most obvious kind. Either things that totally go without saying or complete absences that also go without saying. (e.g. the piano tuner in chapter V).

This is probably the most opaque poem in the collection so I'll do my best to gloss it. Didn't Abraham Lincoln live in a log cabin? In any case, the narrator of this poem is the same one as in 'I am no Longer Your Pilot' from *Harbour Beyond the Movie* wherein a pig falls out of the sky ('tedious and twee'—Laura Steele, *Intercapillary Space*) who resigns himself to life in a log cabin, far away from magazine publishers and issues of national identity and gender. I've always loved the image of the log cabin—it's one of those objects I like putting in poems just because I think it *looks* good, made of logs, surrounded by snow. Sigh. Most of the poets I really enjoy have a cavalier attitude to subject matter—in so far as they actually have an imagination.

Skiff? That's stupid. Should have put bob-sleigh or cable car or something.

I've pretty much sworn off writing about books that don't exist now. *The Raspberry Paradox* is a fairytale I wrote about a depressed princess and her suitors—all of whom are competing for her hand in marriage via trying to make her smile. The main character asks the princess what would make her happiest and she answers, 'Bring me a wave from the ocean!' So the suitor gets all of his servants to build a pewter trough two miles long and marches it down to the beach where he orders it dipped into the sea to catch a wave. Then he takes it back to the Princess's room and orders it poured over the floor, where it just lies as a foot-deep puddle of salt water and seaweed. Which is a lovely metaphor for things being ephemeral. Laura Steele is right about me.

II.

'I think you are drafted [. . .] lousily on purpose.' A reference to *Thus Spake Zarathustra*, Nietzsche (1909). As Zarathustra descends the mountain the first man he encounters is a 'saint', among whose statements is the following: 'Now I love God: men I do not love. Man is a thing too imperfect for me. Love to man would be fatal to me.' (p. 5) Which, sure, would be a perfectly noble cause for Z. to argue against, if it vaguely approximated the actual ethos of any saint on record, who, if my research is anything to go by, tend to love mankind in spite of its imperfection—which is kind of the point of Christianity, no?

This is like early tabloid journalism—you want to bring something down, make sure you take the crassest, dumbest manifestation of that something. And if it doesn't exist, make it up; you control the means of representation. Everyone is cynical and nobody really has any integrity—apart from tabloid journalists, naturally. Create a cliché then mock it for being a cliché. So if you want to take a pot-shot at something, try to take it at the most beautiful, wise manifestation of that something then see how pleased you feel with yourself.

The other man prying on the conversation is just there to deflate the narrator's sense of wonder that anybody should ever talk about such things. We live in pretty unexamined times. Anti-intellectualism often poses as class-protest (and they certainly don't care about your *actual* background). Steve's defeatist letter suggests that in times of war, the artist and her natural predator live in a state of universal exile, failing to build a fire.

III.

'You'd better make sure we don't get bored today!' This letter is a veiled criticism from Steve—who is living in the war-torn city below. Although actually, there's probably nothing more tedious than huddling, terrified, in a corner. In peace-time, there's something pleasurable in having nothing to do for a whole day—not even anything fun—except for eat three times and clean up afterwards. Every minor task takes on a critical intensity. Some of my favourite weekends have passed like that.

Sometimes you should just sit there and appreciate the fact that you're not in the army.

Around here it gets totally opaque and I'm just leaving ideas half explained or less—which is either unbearably pretentious or the soul of poetry. Not sure. 'It wasn't a dream,' is a straightforward falsehood as the character uttering it has apparently just woken from a dream (again, the simplistic contradictions). However, it could also be taken as an assertion that, rather than a dream, it was a vision. The stone—which will 'grant less pleasure and kindle more desire' is supposed to be a beautiful stone that people can get addicted simply to looking at. (I'm sure I've stolen this from somewhere, but I can't remember where). So it stands in for any addiction—the diminishing returns inversely proportional to the need for more. This isn't exactly clear from the poem itself, but hey, it's a character describing her half-remembered dream, so it wouldn't be. The reappearance of the parasol indicates that the philosophers have been eaten by wolverines, but you got that already, right?

IV.

The perpetual motion dolls: an utterly self-indulgent dream-narrative. A recurring nightmare I've had for years. The dream is just like the poem. I get back to our flat to find that my partner has installed five horrible dolls. The other three: 1. A Lieutenant with an axe. A tremor runs through the axe every five seconds—other than that, he is still. 2. A man who looks not unlike me, although cruelly caricatured. He performs a silly dance, waving his arms and legs—his spine is attached to a supporting pole. 3. A headless man in Jacobean dress. His hands keep moving up to his absent head, then falling back suddenly.

The Agnostic Temple echoes with the emptiness motif. Vague analogy: somebody who can't choose between prose and poetry. Also, the question of who is speaking: the idea that we are always supposed to understand the rhetorical device the writer is relying on, that we are always supposed to be on their side, whatever they're covertly denigrating—even if it happens to be our own creed. The crasser the writing, the more offensive this assumption feels. The sermon: suspicion of tradition. Protestant/Catholic tensions I was working through. Also a reflection on the absurd pretence of revolution that sometimes afflicts poetry—the prose poem in particular. Actually, maybe I was being sincere—in a 'rip it up and start again' sense. I'm no fan of Eliot's Great Tradition—which seems to have left us with lots and lots of really boring poems *about* old famous poets. Thanks a lot, keepers of the flame. No answer to the narrator's question. Again, the emptiness—the question without an answer, a conversation with someone asleep.

V.

I think I cribbed 'committing enormities' from *Crime and Punishment*. It's now used predominantly to refer to vastness as opposed to things indescribably terrible in nature. One of those facts about English usage I'd read in a book recently and pretended to have known all along. Out of everything I've ever written, I'm proudest of the Charlie Brown / broken wheelbarrow analogy. I've always been a huge fan of *Peanuts*.

'It is all very well to argue about solipsism, but what about the likes of us who don't know what the word solipsism means?' Again, issues of anti-intellectualism: the idea that even using certain words makes you somehow elitist. Oh, yeah, because dictionaries are only sold to the elite, right? What I think works here, if anything, is the contradiction: There's something solipsistic

in remaining wilfully ignorant about what solipsism means. However, the letter purports to be from a collective voice of the 'ordinary people' in the city below the mountain—when it is actually by Steve, so it is really Steve's caricature.

VI.

There's more collage stuff going on here—and elsewhere in this poem: 'The material world is progressing endlessly in a series of cycles.'—and that kind of thing. This is something that experimental poetry does an awful lot—lists of joke-aphorisms designed to point out that aphorisms are a bit pompous, etc. I suppose I'd been influenced. Most of the collage stuff here comes from theories of the natural world in which the human race is reduced to a minor irritation in an environment that would be better off without it—a sort of whole-species inferiority complex.

Black and White soup could be: 1. Soup in an old movie. 2. Soup that contains a bizarre mixture of oils that give it a chequered appearance, even after stirring. Also it just sounds like a soup company—like Crosse and Blackwell. I got the name from a friend. He was eating a bacon and egg sandwich late one night. Some of us asked him what he was eating. He said, 'This here's Black and White soup,' in an American accent—and it stayed with me.

VII.

Full lyrics to Steve's song:

Liar, liar, lie
Liar, liar, lie
Liar, liar, lie

Liar, liar, lie
Liar, liar, lie.

A dirty grey feather isn't quite a white feather, but it's halfway there—thus symbolising Steve's ambivalent attitude towards his half-brother. Maybe this is instrumental in the narrator's decision to go out and find Nicola at the end of the poem.

VIII.

Maya = mistaking the map for the territory. In the first edition I had 'pinuckle' instead of 'pinochle', the card game to which I was trying to refer. I don't know why I didn't look it up before putting it in wrong. What an idiot.

The final exchange is an attempt at hard-boiled dialogue, neither character saying what they mean. Steve expresses his desire for the narrator not to risk his life by inviting him to play cards; the narrator expresses his determination to save Nicola through not being able to hold playing cards while wearing gloves—which is ridiculous as he could just take the gloves off. But, you know, he's pretending to be a tough guy and doesn't want to give anyone a chance to change his mind.

EPILOGUE

Slices of hamburger meat in grease proof paper is something from Steinbeck's *The Grapes of Wrath*. I hope it's clear enough that this epilogue is a *prequel* to the chapters of the poem, depicting, as it does, the first meeting between the narrator and Nicola in the supermarket—three years ago or thereabouts (c.f. chapter VI). So essentially this is just a love story. Nothing avant-garde about that.

Scarecrow

Full text of the judge's closing statement: 'What a foul creature stands before us as would defile the closest thing we have to a relic. To call his act unnatural does not go far enough; it is blasphemy and animism with intent to corrupt. Thus the halcyon meadows of our youth go to seed and become the hotbed of many improprieties; though the wall between right and wrong be porous, let us keep it, on the whole, intact.'

The Wolf's Career

I.

The wolf's sermon is similar to the Agnostic sermon in 'Log Cabin'. I've heard several people say 'What's wrong with being elitist?' in public forums and go on to define 'elite' as simply referring to the best example of a given thing—which I think sort of misses the point; it's more about where you're looking for those examples. However, I often use 'fear of elitism' as an excuse not to learn or do something, as in, 'I can't read Proust; people on the bus might think I'm elitist.' The Wolf's Prayer is actually the end of 'The Journalist's Prayer'—a poem I was writing at the time which seemed to fit the mood of the piece. Luther himself started a peasant's revolt, but it was sort of an accident and not really what he had in mind. Luther was the one who translated the bible into German—published in 1543.

II.

Ah, 'chimerical'. I've been misusing that word for years. Annabelle is the girlfriend from the first Wolf poem. She is also the woman being searched for in 'Daughters of the Lonesome Isle' (which is dedicated *to Annabelle*—although she doesn't actually exist—and the mysterious stranger in 'Film Noir'.)

III.

I remember a guest assembly at my school from a motorcyclist who had been dispatched, presumably, to scare the hell out of us so that we'd drive safely when we were old enough to learn. Among the fun facts he impressed upon us was the statistic that one in six of us was going to die in a car accident. 'And you're all sitting there thinking, "It's not going to be me,"' he said. 'Well that's your *first* mistake.' We exchanged worried glances. As the assembly continued, I occupied myself working out a brief tally, based on the other sure-fire statistics I knew, (1 in 3 will get cancer, 1 in 4 experience severe mental illness, 1 in 20 boy's voices will never break, etc.) and the outlook didn't look too good—in fact we were all certainly going to die. Of course, the kid you *really* had to feel sorry for was the impotent squeaky-voiced obsessive-compulsive with skin *and* lung cancer who was going to drive fatally into a tree shortly after his fifth marriage failed.

IV.

Those really are Goethe's last recorded words—which is apposite because he was totally obsessed with light.

V.

In the first edition I had the portholes of light 'gliding over your iris and into your cornea'. For some reason I thought the tear ducts of your eyes were called corneas—I think because I half over-heard a grizzly radio news item about people harvesting corneas and I assumed (again, I'm not sure why) that this was just the swanky name for tear duct. So instead of looking it up in an anatomy book (and my wife is an occupational therapist, so there's always one to hand, albeit a really heavy one), I just went ahead with my inexplicable misunderstanding. The cornea is actually the outermost layer of the eye. Of course, that never would have been published back in the day when poetry books had military and medical editors. Tear duct sounds much nicer in the sentence anyway.

VI.

This isn't based on an existing play—more a type. Somebody really did once try to sell me a toaster in a park in Bristol.

VII.

The only word which cannot be included in a riddle is the answer to that riddle: e.g. a riddle to which the answer is 'Pie' couldn't include the word pie. Salman Rushdie said that V. S. Naipaul's *The Enigma of Arrival* is a novel-length riddle to which the answer is 'Love'. Therefore, the narrator, having been pointedly excluded from the wolf's letter, tries to comfort himself with the thought that the wolf may see him as the answer to a riddle he has constructed. However, as the riddle here seems to concern the descent of man into mediocrity, it is hardly a riddle to which one would want to be the answer.

The Esplanade

I.

'The Esplanade' takes place in the city below the hermit's mountain in 'Log Cabin'. The narrator is an assassin who has been engaged by the city to kill the spy *Red Fox and his Canoe*. *Red Fox and his Canoe* is actually the name of an American children's novel, listed on the back of *Mouse Soup* (the author isn't cited). I guess you could call this *collage*. It just struck me as a great name for an agent—c.f. Le Carré's *Tinker Taylor Soldier Spy*. They always seem to be playing around with nursery rhymes and children's fiction, as if the juxtaposition with their manly feats of espionage sort of adds to the mystique. So why not a spy named after the *full title* of a kid's book? Don't answer that.

The writer/travel writer stuff looks really clumsy now—even though I only wrote it two years ago. The three characters are 1. A tourist with a type-writer; 2. a novelist; 3. a travel-writer; all vying for attention and authenticity, all attempting to use their exotic location to achieve this and all failing utterly and turning on one another. Where exactly I get off thinking I'm better than them is anyone's guess. Maybe because I have a gun.

'*DEATH TO ALL EXTREMISTS*': At this point I kept hearing people on call-in shows saying: 'What I think we should do is round up all the extremists and put them on an island and blow them up and let the rest of the world get on with their lives.' Which is fair enough, but, you know, a tad extremist.

II.

It's only just struck me how disgusting an accompaniment crème de menthe would be to calamari.

III.

'A beast that wants discourse of reason would have mourned longer' is from my favourite *Hamlet* soliloquy, Act I Sc. II. I have set it to music (D / C / G / Em) and regularly sing it when left alone in the flat. The butler is a metonym for servitude: better to serve drinks than to serve a ridiculously convoluted espionage agency.

I worked in a beautiful second-hand bookshop for two years. It was my favourite job and paid better than the meat packing factory. Because the money was kept in a little tin, a customer having the correct change was a matter of great importance.

The stylistic device in this poem was going to be this kind of syntactical spoonerism, whereby 'I'll watch him like a hawk' becomes 'I'll hawk him like a watch'—'hawk' as in to sell, e.g. taking a watch to a pawn shop. Once again, applying this with any consistency seemed trite and overdetermined, so it only appears a couple of times in the final cut.

IV.

Actually I suppose the butler was a spy too, only he was dressed as a butler. The game of chess is supposed to hint at how tenuous any sense of right and wrong becomes once you enter into a double, treble or quadruple cross; and the world's ultimate indifference is symbolised by the concierge who is only doing his job.

V.

The narrator has befriended Jorge, the owner of the shoe shop on top of which he has been stationed, to the point of actually supporting his business—even though the shoes Jorge makes are ridiculous. This shows that the narrator is a very nice man who has, nevertheless, been forced to take action due to the atrocities perpetrated by the other side (the TWAPATTCAR) to whom belongs *Red Fox and his Canoe*.

VI.

I had recently bought a bottle of Retsina for the first time, not realising Retsina tastes like pine needles. The pots and pans being bashed but unused are a metaphor for an argument which goes through the motions of open debate, like most radio interviews with politicians. The last words of *Red Fox and his Canoe* and the governor are cribbed / paraphrased from conversations I had with a college room-mate who was training for the armed forces.

VII.

Plus, he *literally* has a heavy hand, because it's made of glass! Ha ha ha!

The 'damning' scene refers to the 1930s sci-fi (which in this case is short for science-financial) romp *An Itinerant Carpenter in Purgatory* by Lucille Priscian-Head—concerning a future in which people are forced to complete endlessly repetitive menial tasks in exchange for 'credits'—which can be exchanged for goods and services. The main character doesn't arrive until the last page and there are several instances of damnation whereby a character unwittingly consigns another, bodily, to 'hell' simply by verbally damning them. 'Anita examined the charred carpet where Charles had stood. "Charles?" she said. "Charles? This isn't funny."' (p. 67) No explanation is given for this device, as if none were needed, but it leads to a greater number of devils—and the reader is unsure whether they only exist in the given character's head or not.

VIII.

Phlox is one of those words I never want to see again. I don't have anything against county councillors *per se*—the good ones work very hard for their communities for scant reimbursement—but at the time I wrote this poem there was a specific county councillor I had in mind, who has since been ousted for being evil. Hooray for democracy!

'How easy to suggest that all is meaningless . . .' Don't you think quite a lot of writers do just that? Existentialism without the lapsed-Catholicism to give it some sparkle (the only reason Sartre is any fun whatsoever). Shouldn't you be out bringing down gazelles with your bare hands?

EPILOGUE

At this point the narrator has befriended the butler (who was already visibly on his side) and Emily, the fake wife of Red Fox and his Canoe, who has turned out to be a double-agent. They talk about *The Cloud of Unknowing* and early-church mystics—the narrator remains silent as he is traumatised and can now only communicate through having tea poured over his head. The war continues. Anarchists are recruited by fashion magazines. 'Is anger murder? Then murder isn't so bad!'

Lightning Source UK Ltd.
Milton Keynes UK
UKOW03f1030060617
302767UK00003B/276/P